Can These Bones Live?

Contemporary Dramas for Lent and Easter
David H. Kehret

Augsburg Fortress
Minneapolis

CAN THESE BONES LIVE?
Contemporary Dramas for Lent and Easter

Cover Design: Barsuhn Design
Cover Art: Markell Studios
Editors: Dennis Bushkofsky and Rebecca Lowe

Manufactured in the U.S.A.

ISBN 0-8066-3965-2   3-3965

03   02   01   00   99   1   2   3   4   5

Contents

Welcome . . .

to *Can These Bones Live? Contemporary Dramas for Lent and Easter.* Centuries ago, the Christian church began to use drama to present biblical stories, often communicating Christian messages to those who had no access to the written word. Contemporary Christian drama presents the gospel in ways that deeply affect people, often piercing through the shells and shields that can hold people at a distance from scripture. *Can These Bones Live?* provides a new set of dramas for parish use based on the liturgical readings from Lent, Holy Week, and Easter.

Appropriate in any year

The three-year cycle of the Revised Common Lectionary provides the basis for *Can These Bones Live?* This lectionary is similar to other three-year lectionaries used by various denominations. Out of that three-year cycle of readings, the author has selected seven Sundays and holy days with themes common to all three years of Lent, Holy Week, and Easter. Thus, *Can These Bones Live?* provides dramas based on readings for Ash Wednesday, the First Sunday in Lent, Passion Sunday, Maundy Thursday, the Second Sunday of Easter, the Fourth Sunday of Easter, and Pentecost. While the appointed scripture readings for some of these Sundays vary from year to year, the dramas focus on either a central theme or the gospel for the day.

In addition, *Can These Bones Live?* offers a dramatic rendering of five of the primary readings appointed for the Vigil of Easter: Creation, the Flood, the Testing of Abraham, the Exodus, and Ezekiel's Valley of Dry Bones. One or more of these dramas would be appropriate to use during an Easter Vigil service. These five dramas based on Easter Vigil readings could also be used for a midweek Lenten series between Ash Wednesday and Holy Week. Such a series would orient people towards the history of salvation rehearsed each year in the Easter Vigil. The five Easter Vigil dramas, coupled with the dramas for Ash Wednesday and Maundy Thursday, would create a complete midweek Lenten series.

In addition to the listing in the table of contents, the dramas in *Can These Bones Live?* may be used on other Sundays and occasions of the church year, as well. A listing of suggestions based on the Revised Common Lectionary is provided on page 6.

Usable in parishes with rich or lean resources

Parishes with varying degrees of resources will be able to use *Can These Bones Live?* All of the dramas are intended for use within the context of a worship service. Each drama can stand alone or be used in the context of further preaching. No costuming or stage sets are needed. Props are simple and easily obtainable. Some dramas require no props at all.

The five dramas based on readings from the Vigil of Easter require the least resources. Slightly shorter in length than the others, these dramas require only one or two players. Parishes may use the vigil dramas in lieu of the readings. (Most of the other dramas in the book should be used at some point in the service following their respective readings.) Two of the vigil dramas provide the option of using either one or two cast members. Only one vigil drama requires two persons. None of these five dramas requires props other than a reading stand. Staging is simple, and the scripts could actually be read rather than memorized. On the other hand, someone with theater experience could bring a rich and deep expression to the characters portrayed in the short monologues.

Six of the dramas for specific Sundays and holy days are slightly longer and more intricate, calling for three to seven players. A few simple props are required and some effort at staging is necessary. While any of these dramas could be done as readers theater, they come alive most fully when time and effort is devoted to memorization of lines and thorough rehearsal.

The dramatic reading of the passion stands in a separate category by itself. Designed to replace the reading of the passion gospel on Passion Sunday or on Good Friday, it is conceived as a presentation that church drama groups should read rather than memorize or stage.

Several dramas include phonetic spelling of words to assist actors with pronunciation. Following is a pronunciation guide.

syllable:	as in:	syllable:	as in:
ah	water	aw	awe
a	cat	uh	dull
eh	net	ih	sit
ee	feet	ay	day
oh	boat	ai	ice
oo	boot		

David H. Kehret
Valparaiso, Indiana

Copyright permission

This book includes permission to reproduce the scripts and use them in local (not-for-profit) church uses. Please be sure to include the copyright acknowledgements found at the bottom of the first page of each script. If you have any questions about this permission or wish to use the plays in another context, please contact the publisher.

Additional Suggestions for Use
Based on the Revised Common Lectionary

Drama Title	*Appointed Reading*	*Calendar Day*
Deliverance	(Genesis 1:1—2:4a) (1:1-5) (1:1-5, 26-31)	Holy Trinity, Year A Baptism of Our Lord, Year B St. John, Apostle and Evangelist
Rainbows	(Genesis 9:8-17)	First Sunday in Lent, Year B
Heartbreak	(Genesis 22:1-14)	Sunday between June 26 and July 2, Proper 8, Year A
Freedom	(Exodus 14:19-31)	Sunday between Sept. 11 and 17, Proper 19, Year A
Can These Bones Live?	(Ezekiel 37:1-14)	Fifth Sunday in Lent, Year A Day of Pentecost, Year B
Window on God	(Psalm 23)	Fourth Sunday of Lent, Year A Sunday between July 17 and 23, Proper 11, Year B Sunday between Oct. 9 and 15, Proper 23, Year A
Waiting	(Acts 1:1-11) (1:6-14) (1:15-17, 21-26) (1:15-26) (2:14a, 22-32) (2:14a, 36-41) (2:42-47)	Ascension of Our Lord Seventh Sunday of Easter, Year A Seventh Sunday of Easter, Year B St. Matthias, Apostle Second Sunday of Easter, Year A Third Sunday of Easter, Year A Fourth Sunday of Easter, Year A

Dust

Ash Wednesday
Joel 2:15-16

Duration: 10 minutes.

Cast: Three men and three women. Players form a line or a slight arc across the front of the worship space in the following order:

Man: 1   Woman: 2   Man: 3   Woman: 4   Woman: 5   Man: 6

Players do "speech chorus" sections from the line position, coming down front as needed for the short scenarios, then returning to the line.

Props: One prop is necessary: a piece of off-white cloth, three feet by nine feet. The cloth is folded up at the beginning and end, and during the drama becomes a dust cloth, a funeral pall, and finally a folded shroud. Two other props are useful: an envelope with several sheets of paper inside and a Bible.

1: Remember!

2-4-6: Remember that you are dust!

ALL: Remember that you are dust and to dust you shall return!

1: Blow the trumpet in Zion!

4: Sanctify a fast!

6: Call a solemn assembly!

3: Gather the people!

ALL: Remember!

5: Dust!

ALL: Remember!

1: Hello!

4: Hello, Mr. Johnson?

1: Yes.

4: This is Dr. Weller's office calling.

1: Oh, hello Dr. Weller.

4: No, this is not Dr. Weller. This is his office calling.

1: Oh…Yes?

4: We are calling about the results of the tests you took on Monday.

1: Monday. Yes, the lab tests.

4: Right. The results are here and…

1: How did they turn out?

4: Well, Doctor would like you to schedule an appointment as soon as possible so he can go over things with you.

1: Sure thing. The week after next is pretty…

4: No, Mr. Johnson. Dr. Weller would really like me to set something up with you sooner than that.

1: Sooner. Well, next week is a real bear, but I suppose I could squeeze…

4: Doctor is suggesting this week at the latest.

1: This week yet?

4: Yes, preferably tomorrow.

1: Tomorrow? I don't see why there's such… *(fumbles for word)*

4: "Urgency," Mr. Johnson? That's the word Doctor used. He said, "Stress to Mr. Johnson the urgency of him seeing me immediately."

1: Urgency…Tomorrow? Let me get my calendar.

2-3-5-6: Remember!

6: Blow the trumpet in Zion!

2: Remember that you are dust!

3: Sanctify a fast!

ALL: Remember!

5: *(snaps the folded cloth as if shaking it out)*

6: *(coughs and waves hand in front of his face)*

5: Dust!

ALL: Remember!

4: *(opening envelope, fumbling)*

5: What's that? What did you get?

4: It's from the state. It's the results from that certification exam I took. I can't believe it has taken them so long to process it. You know how hard I worked to get ready for it! Finally! *(reading, getting very sober)*

5: So? What does it say? Huh?

4: I don't want to talk about it.

5: Come on, tell me what it says.

4: Leave me alone.

5: You didn't pass? Oh, Julie, you studied so hard. This meant so much to you. It must be a mistake. They got you mixed up with someone else.

4: I don't think so. This looks pretty official to me. Name, social security number, etc. We regret to inform you that…

5: *(reads along)* Oh, but it says you can try again. There's a whole list of test dates.

4: This was already the third time.

5: But each time you probably get better and better at it.

4: It's a different test each time.

5: Oh.

4: Well, this is a new twist! This time they sent along a flier for a vocational guidance seminar.

5: That doesn't sound like such a bad idea. Maybe you need to explore where you're going.

4: I don't want to "explore where I'm going." I just want to get there.

5: Maybe this is not right for you.

4: After all the work I've put in? Of course it's right for me.

5: Maybe it just isn't you.

4: If this is not what I am, then who am I?

1-2-3-6: Remember!

2: Remember that you are dust!

ALL: Remember!

4: When the Sabbath was over…

ALL: Remember!

3: And to dust you shall return!

ALL: Remember!

6: Dust!

3: Remember the good old days, the fun we had, the things we did.

2: I can't live in the past.

3: I just want things to be like they used to be.

2: But I'm not who I used to be. I've changed. You've changed.

3: Not that much.

2: I don't know you anymore, Roger. I don't know the person I'm married to.

3: I think I still know you.

2: No you don't! I don't even know who I am anymore. Life is whizzing by. The years drop away. I've changed. You've changed, no doubt about that! Who are we?

3: We didn't have to ask questions like that when we were first together. We just celebrated life.

2: Maybe we should have been asking questions about who we were and where we were going. I'm not sure we knew. Now we're just drifting on habit and routine. I'm tired of not knowing who I am or who I am married to or where life is taking us.

3: Don't you think questions like that could wait until we're…

2: Wait for what? Wait until we're dead? Great! I'm not satisfied with that. And I need someone who is willing to ask those questions with me!

3: What does that mean?

2: It means that I need you, Roger, to want to know who you are and to want to know who I am, and for us together to ask serious questions about where we are going. Where *we* are going, Roger, and maybe even what we are supposed to be here for.

3: Maybe it is overdue. Maybe it's too late.

2: Not too late.

3: Together?

2: Together.

1-4-5-6: Remember!

2-4-5: Call a solemn assembly.

4: When the Sabbath was over Mary Magdalene, and Mary the Mother of James…

ALL: Remember!

1-3-5: Sanctify the congregation!

5: Remember that you are *(snaps the cloth)*

6: *(coughing)* I wish you would stop that.

5: Just shaking it out. Open the window and let some fresh air in. It's spring. Time to clean house.

6: What?

5: Spring cleaning. Here, help me move some things. You're home early.

6: I'm really not in the mood for spring cleaning.

5: What's wrong? Why are you home early?

6: I needed to get away. You're not the only one cleaning house.

5: Oh, you've decided to clean your office?

6: No. They have decided to clean out the office.

5: What? What are you talking about?

6: Another division merger. Another downsizing for efficiency. The word just came down.

5: And what does that mean for you?

6: I don't know. Nobody knows yet. Everybody's scared.

5: Well, we've weathered this situation before.

6: I suppose so.

5: What do you mean 'You suppose so?' Just because it was my company five years ago, that doesn't count?

6: No, I didn't mean it that way. I just don't want to go through it again.

5: I know. It was a hard time. Maybe having it behind us puts it in perspective. It did make us ask a lot of questions we had been avoiding.

6: There's got to be some way to ask important questions about life without being up against the wall.

1-2-3-4: Remember!

2: Dust!

3: Sanctify a fast!

ALL: Remember!

4: When the Sabbath was over, Mary Magdalene, and Mary the mother of James, and Salome bought spices, so that they might go and anoint him.

ALL: Remember!

1: Blow the trumpet in Zion!

5: Call a solemn assembly!

6: Gather the people!

ALL: Remember!

(Players pick up the cloth and spread it out. Then, three on each side, grasping the cloth six inches from its edge, they carry it like a pall-covered coffin down the start of the center aisle. Slowly and carefully, they lower it as into an open grave. Then they gather around the "grave." 3 positions himself as a worship leader, picking up the Bible from a convenient location and using it as a prayer book.)

3: We are gathered here to remember Arthur Johnson, taken from us in the midst of life—husband, father, brother, and friend. Earth to earth, ashes to ashes, dust to dust.

(Each player in turns goes to comfort 4. After greeting 4, 1 and 2 carefully fold up the pall, folding it in half lengthwise three times, then once in half crosswise. 2 carries it.)

1: He was a good man.

2: We'll always remember him.

5: I'm so sorry things turned out like this.

6: He went so fast.

3: *(gives the Bible to 4)* Let me know if there's anything I can do for you.

(After marking cross on foreheads, players return to the line.)

1: *(marking cross on forehead of 3)* Remember!

3: *(marking cross on 5)* Remember!

5: *(marking cross on 2)* Remember!

2: *(marking cross on 6)* Remember! *(As she goes back to the line, 2 carefully places the folded shroud in a visible place at the front of the worship space, leaving it there after the drama is over.)*

6: *(marking cross on 4)* Remember!

4: *(reading from Bible)* When the Sabbath was over, Mary Magdalene, and Mary the mother of James, and Salome bought spices, so that they might go and anoint him.

And very early on the first day of the week, when the sun had risen, they went to the tomb. They had been saying to one another, "Who will roll away the stone for us?"

ALL: *(softly)* Remember!

Debriefing

First Sunday in Lent
Matthew 4:1-11; Mark 1:9-15; Luke 4:1-13

Duration: 11 minutes.

Setting: The wilderness.

Cast: Three "evil" spirits, who do not deserve the courtesy of being given names. They are hostile, mean, sarcastic, selfish, and self-centered beings. Nothing about them is endearing. Their speech is always nearly a snarl and always dramatic. To get from place to place they swirl around. Some good dramatic coaching would help to create the effect.

Props and costumes: None. Please, no "Halloween devils."

> *(Two SPIRITS are poised onstage. They are inactive, but "hovering" over the scene. The third, SPIRIT 1, swirls onstage to a short distance away from the other two spirits.)*

SPIRIT 1: *(claps hands sharply)* We have to meet!

SPIRIT 2: Yeah, yeah, yeah.

SPIRIT 1: Now! Immediately!

SPIRIT 3: Why? What's up?

SPIRIT 1: It didn't work out; that's what's up! A total bust!

SPIRIT 3: Impossible!

SPIRIT 2: I don't believe it!

SPIRIT 1: I just ran into B. L. coming in from the wilderness. He is fit to be tied. You know how he can be!

SPIRIT 3: But, it was his idea in the first place!

SPIRIT 1: His idea, maybe, but we're the ones who worked out the details. Therefore, we are the ones who get the blame! All he needed was one—fool-proof—temptation. We gave him three just to be safe, and he came up with zip. Jesus is out there in the wilderness this very minute being ministered to by angels.

SPIRIT 2: I hate angels!

SPIRIT 3: I can't stand angels!

SPIRIT 1: You're just jealous! Stop feeling sorry for yourself! We have more important things to worry about. B. L. will be after our hides.

SPIRIT 2: I don't see how my temptation could have failed. It was an old, tried-and-true, classic temptation. It has always worked. There was nothing experimental about it.

SPIRIT 1: Didn't you hear me? None of them worked, and we're going to have to figure out a way to defend ourselves.

(The three SPIRITS swirl away from each other in different directions. They cannot stand being with each other and they cannot stand being apart from each other. Slowly they converge again.)

SPIRIT 3: *(accusing SPIRIT 2)* Your big idea about Jesus jumping off the roof of the temple was a failure from the start.

SPIRIT 2: Oh, you think so? All B. L. had to do was suggest to Jesus that, as he is the Son of God, God would protect him. Would God want to see an investment wiped out prematurely? So that gave Jesus some real leverage, which is what we've been seeking all along. He could launch things with a spectacular sign: floating down from the roof of the temple to a safe landing in the middle of an admiring crowd below. And if he shied back from jumping, it would show that he was chicken and didn't trust God. A classic double bind. Either he uses God for his own purposes or he doesn't trust God. There's no other way out. Either way, we win. It couldn't fail.

SPIRIT 3: But it did! Don't you understand—it was a lousy idea! All Jesus had to do was quote the commandment: "You shall not put the Lord your God to the test," and he was off the hook.

SPIRIT 2: We didn't expect him to do that!

SPIRIT 1: *(sarcastically)* Oh, "We didn't expect him to do that!" But we were supposed to expect the unexpected. It's not going to go down easy with B. L.

SPIRIT 2: *(addressing SPIRIT 1)* And your idea of taking Jesus up the mountain and promising him the world if he would just worship B.L? Talk about crazy ideas!

SPIRIT 1: Not so crazy! It's got a solid history. Look at all the governors and the emperors and the presidents and the senators we have in our pocket. It just sounds crazy. In reality, it works.

SPIRIT 2: Not this time it didn't!

SPIRIT 3: Turning stones into bread had a lot going for it. My idea, matter of fact. Subtle. Has to do with survival. Everyone has an instinct for survival, and Jesus had been on a forty-day fast. Turning stones into bread wouldn't hurt anybody. All he had to do was use his power to provide a little something for himself. No problem! After he did it once, it would be easy to tempt him to do it again and again and again and again until his whole purpose in life would be turned into looking out for "Number One." Except, he could not know that at the start.

SPIRIT 2: He didn't fall for it! I'm not sure what went wrong, but nothing worked!

(The SPIRITS "hover" circling around each other.)

SPIRIT 3: So, why does B. L. have such a thing about this guy? There are lots of other fish in the sea.

SPIRIT 1: Listen, from that moment down by the Jordan when the voice from heaven said, "This is my beloved Son," I knew Mr. B. L. Zebub was going to be hooked. That's the title B. L. has wanted from the start! Pure, pure, pure envy. I just knew he would be out to get this guy!

SPIRIT 3: So, B. L. is bent out of shape, which means he isn't going to be fun to be around, to say the least. But what difference is it going to make in the bigger picture?

SPIRIT 1: You're probably right. Everybody else is still falling for our tricks lock, stock, and barrel. *(laughs hideously)* Look on the bright side of things. I have this emperor in Rome who has bought into ruling over the world. He has traded everything for it—family, colleagues, even personal satisfaction. He will never be content, because he keeps discovering another piece of the world that's not under his control. And as soon as he puts it under his control something else slips away. He pretends to be a god and wants to have everybody think of him as a god. Hasn't the faintest idea who he has had to worship to get where he is. Delicious!

SPIRIT 2: You think that's impressive? You think you deserve some award for landing a big fish? I've got thousands upon thousands of people doing the very same thing in their own families. Any suggestion that people can be more than human has a future. It's worked from the very beginning. It will always work.

SPIRIT 3: Not nearly as well as the Bread Gambit, which we can pull off using anything handy. As long as we can convince people that something they want is something they need, there's no end to the possibilities. You can drag them around anywhere. There's more general distress—not to mention delightful wars and oppression—available down that road than by getting someone to want to rule the world. It works! Which is more than you can say for your "roof of the temple" thing!

SPIRIT 2: Not so fast, there. The "roof of the temple leap" may be more subtle, but it's a natural. Like you said, people want to be more than human and invulnerable. They want to have life always work out, and they don't want to be responsible for their own choices. When life isn't like that, they blame God. They go around saying, "If there was a God…" or "If God really cared.…" They do it without needing to be prompted. Now and then, we can push it into something really big and cause misery far exceeding our efforts.

SPIRIT 1: Then all our temptations have a solid future! I can already imagine the variations we can evolve as the centuries go on. It gives me the shivers.

(The three SPIRITS turn in upon themselves in shivering delight, until reality and terror breaks through.)

SPIRIT 3: But will that be good enough for B.L? He had his heart set on snaring this guy. He's such a control freak. You think he might be looking to us for some new ideas?

SPIRIT 1: I think he has given up on us. He was talking about developing an insider among the folks who gather around Jesus. Don't quite know what he has in mind.

SPIRIT 2: You think he might know something about Jesus that we don't know?

SPIRIT 3: Yeah, I've been worrying about that, too. What if this resistance to temptation starts to spread?

SPIRIT 2: I wouldn't worry about that. Over the centuries we've seen any number of righteous people, whose names we all despise. But has it ever caught on? Never!

SPIRIT 3: Remember the panic we were in when God gave the Law to Moses? We thought that with the law put in writing it was all over for us. Guess again! Didn't change a thing; just made people more miserable knowing they were doing something wrong. I wouldn't sweat it!

SPIRIT 1: But we still don't know what God is up to with this guy, Jesus. Never trust God to play fair. What if Jesus stays clean the whole way through, and God decides that's good enough to cover for the whole human race? Makes our future kind of pointless—amusing maybe, but pointless.

SPIRIT 2: So, who's going to tell B. L. that's a possibility? Not me!

SPIRIT 3: Don't look at me!

SPIRIT 1: Not on your life! You've seen what he does to bearers of bad news. Let him figure it out for himself!

(The SPIRITS circle each other for a moment, then swirl away into the wilderness.)

The Passion of Our Lord Jesus Christ

Based Upon the Gospel Accounts of Matthew, Mark, and Luke

Duration: 15 minutes.

Cast: Six readers. One will read the words of Jesus throughout. The others will serve as narrators for the five sections, as well as providing the other voice parts.

Woman: 1   Man: 2   Man: 3   Woman: 4   Man: 5   Jesus

(This meditation on the Passion of Our Lord begins with the singing of stanza one of "My Song is Love Unknown." The text is by Samuel Crossman (1624–1683). Two tunes are commonly used: RHOSYMEDRE *and* LOVE UNKNOWN. *This and subsequent stanzas may be sung by congregation, choir, or a soloist throughout the reading.)*

(Sing:)
My song is love unknown,
My Savior's love to me,
Love to the loveless shown,
That they might lovely be.
Oh, who am I, that for my sake
My Lord should take frail flesh and die?

THE CONSPIRACY AGAINST JESUS (Mark 14:1-2; Matt. 26:14-16)

NAR.(1): Two days before the Festival of Passover and Unleavened Bread, the chief priests and the scribes were looking for a way to arrest Jesus secretly and kill him.

2: Not during the Festival, or the people may riot.

NAR.(1): One of the twelve, Judas Iscariot, went to the chief priests.

JUDAS (3): What will you give me to place him into your hands?

NAR.(1): They promised Judas thirty pieces of silver, and he began to look for an opportunity to betray Jesus.

THE LAST SUPPER (Luke 22:7-8, 14; Matt. 26:26-30)

NAR.(1): On the day of Unleavened Bread, when the Passover lamb was killed, Jesus sent Peter and John.

JESUS: Go and prepare the Passover for us to eat.

NAR.(1): They went and found everything as Jesus had told them; and they prepared the Passover. When everything was ready, Jesus sat down with the apostles.

During the meal, Jesus took the bread. He spoke a blessing, broke it, and gave it to the disciples.

JESUS: Take, eat; this is my body.

NAR.(1): Then he took the cup, gave thanks, and gave it to them.

JESUS: Drink from it, all of you. This is my blood of the new covenant, poured out for many for the forgiveness of sins. Certainly I will not drink of this fruit of the vine again, until I drink it fresh with you in my Father's kingdom.

PETER'S DENIAL FORETOLD (Mark 14:26-31)

NAR.(1): After singing a hymn, they went out to the Mount of Olives.

JESUS: You will all desert me tonight, for it is written, "I will strike the shepherd, and the sheep will be scattered." But after I am raised up, I will go before you to Galilee.

PETER (5): Even though all desert you, I will not.

JESUS: Peter, I tell you, this very night, before the cock crows twice, you will deny me three times.

PETER (5): *(vehemently)* Even though I must die with you, I will not deny you.

NAR.(1): All of them said the same thing.

> *(Sing:)*
> He came from his blest throne,
> Salvation to bestow;
> But men made strange, and none
> The longed-for Christ would know.
> But, oh, my friend, my friend indeed,
> Who at my need his life did spend!

JESUS PRAYS IN THE GARDEN (Matt. 26:36-46)

NAR.(2): Jesus and the disciples came to a place called Gethsemane.

JESUS: Sit here while I go and pray over there.

NAR.(2): He took along Peter and the two sons of Zebedee, and began to be overcome with grief and anguish.

JESUS: I am overwhelmed with grief; stay here, and keep watch with me.

NAR.(2): Going on a little farther, he fell on the ground and prayed.

JESUS: O my Father, if it is possible, take this cup from me; yet not my will, but your will be done.

NAR.(2): Then he came back to the disciples and found them asleep. He said to Peter:

JESUS: Couldn't you stay awake with me one hour? Watch and pray that you are not tempted; the spirit may be willing, but the flesh is weak.

NAR.(2): Jesus went off a second time and prayed.

JESUS: O my Father, if this cup cannot pass unless I drink it, your will be done.

NAR.(2): Jesus came back and again found them asleep, for their eyes were heavy. So he left them, went away again, and prayed for the third time with the same words. Then he came back to the disciples.

JESUS: Sleeping on? Taking your rest? The time has come for the Son of Man to be betrayed into the hands of sinners. Get up. Let's be on our way. My betrayer is at hand.

JESUS IS TAKEN CAPTIVE (Mark 14:43-50)

NAR.(2): As Jesus was speaking, Judas, one of the twelve, arrived. With him was a crowd bearing swords and clubs, from the chief priests, the scribes, and the elders. The betrayer had set up a signal for them.

JUDAS: The one I will kiss is he; seize him and take him away securely.

NAR.(2): As soon as Judas arrived, he went up to Jesus and said—

JUDAS (3): Rabbi!

NAR.(2): —and kissed him. Then they seized Jesus and held him. But one of those who stood near drew a sword and struck the high priest's slave, cutting off his ear.

JESUS: Did you come out with swords and clubs as though I were a thief? I was with you in the temple teaching day after day, and you did not lay a hand on me. But let the scriptures be fulfilled.

NAR.(2): Then all the disciples deserted him and fled.

(Sing:)
Sometimes they strew his way
And his sweet praises sing;
Resounding all the day
Hosannas to their King.
Then "Crucify!" is all their breath,
And for his death they thirst and cry.

PETER DENIES KNOWING JESUS (Luke 22:54-62)

NAR.(4): They seized Jesus and led him away to the high priest's house. Peter followed at a distance. A fire was kindled in the middle of the courtyard, and they sat down around it, Peter among them. When a servant-girl saw him in the firelight, she stared at him.

GIRL (1): This man was also with him.

PETER (5): Woman, I do not know him.

NAR.(4): A bit later someone else noticed Peter and said:

GIRL (1): Aren't you also one of them?

PETER (5): I am not!

NAR.(4): After about an hour still another insisted.

GIRL (1): I'm sure this man also was with him; for he is a Galilean.

PETER (5): I don't know what you're talking about!

NAR.(4): As he was still speaking, the cock crowed. The Lord turned and looked at Peter. Peter remembered what the Lord had said.

JESUS: Before the cock crows, you will deny me three times.

NAR.(4): Then Peter went out and wept bitter tears.

JESUS ON TRIAL BEFORE THE COUNCIL (Luke 22:63-71)

NAR.(4): At the break of day, the elders of the people, both chief priests and scribes, gathered and brought Jesus to their council.

3: Are you the Messiah? Tell us.

JESUS: If I tell you, you will not believe me; and if I question you, you will not answer me. But from now on the Son of Man will be seated at the right hand of almighty God.

3: Then, are you the Son of God?

JESUS: You say that I am.

3: What further witnesses are needed? We ourselves have heard it from his own lips!

NAR.(4): The men who were holding Jesus began to mock him and beat him; then they blindfolded him and would strike him and ask:

3: Prophesy! Who struck you?

NAR.(4): And they assaulted him in other ways.

JESUS IS TAKEN BEFORE THE ROMAN GOVERNOR (Mark 15:1-5)

NAR.(4): Early morning, the chief priests consulted with the elders and scribes and the whole council. They bound Jesus and led him away to hand him over to Pilate. Pilate asked him:

PILATE (2): Are you the King of the Jews?

JESUS: You say so.

NAR.(4): The chief priests kept on accusing Jesus of many things.

PILATE (2): Don't you have an answer? Look at all their accusations!

NAR.(4): But Jesus did not reply, and Pilate was left wondering.

(Sing:)
Why, what hath my Lord done?
What makes this rage and spite?
He made the lame to run,
He gave the blind their sight.
Sweet injuries! Yet they at these
Themselves displease, and 'gainst him rise.

JESUS IS SENTENCED TO DEATH (Mark 15:6-15)

NAR.(3): During the festival Pilate customarily set free a prisoner for the people, whomever they asked for. A man named Bar-Abbas (bah-RAB-uhs) was in prison with others who had killed people during an insurrection. The crowd came and clamored for Pilate to do his customary release.

PILATE (2): Shall I release for you the King of the Jews?

NAR.(3): Pilate knew that the chief priests had handed Jesus over to him out of jealousy. But the chief priests prompted the crowd to have Pilate release Bar-Abbas for them instead.

PILATE (2): Then what shall I do with the one you call King of the Jews?

1, 4, 5: Crucify him!

PILATE (2): Why, what evil has he done?

1, 4, 5: *(more vehemently)* Crucify him!

NAR.(3): Finally, Pilate, hoping to please the crowd, released Bar-Abbas for them; and after flogging Jesus, he handed Jesus over to be crucified.

JESUS IS BEATEN AND MOCKED (Mark 15:16-20)

NAR.(3): The soldiers led Jesus into the courtyard of the governor's headquarters, and called together their whole company. They put a purple cloak on Jesus, and twisted some thorns into a crown to put on his head. They began saluting him.

5: Hail, King of the Jews!

NAR.(3): They hit him on the head with a stick, spit upon him, and knelt in mock homage before him. Then they stripped off the purple cloak, put his own clothes back on him, and led him out to crucify him.

(Sing:)
They rise, and needs will have
My dear Lord made away;
A murderer they save,
The prince of life they slay.
Yet cheerful he to suffering goes,
That he his foes from thence might free.

JESUS IS CRUCIFIED (Luke 23:33-35; Mark 15:29-30; Luke 23:39-43)

NAR.(5): They came to the place called Calvary and crucified Jesus there, along with criminals on each side of him.

JESUS: Father, forgive them; for they do not know what they are doing.

NAR.(5): And they divided his clothing by casting lots. The people stood by watching; but the leaders derided him.

1: He saved others; let him save himself.

2: If he is indeed God's Messiah, God's chosen one!

NAR.(5): Those who were passing by mocked him, shaking their heads.

1: So, you would destroy the temple and rebuild it in three days?

2: Save yourself. Come down from the cross!

NAR.(5): One of the criminals crucified with him, derided him.

1: You're the Messiah! Save yourself and us!

NAR.(5): But the other rebuked him.

3: Do you not fear God, being under the same sentence of death? And we indeed justly are getting what we deserve. But this man has done nothing wrong. Lord, remember me when you come into your kingdom.

JESUS: Truly, you will be with me today in Paradise.

JESUS DIES ON THE CROSS (Mark 15:33-36; Luke 23:46-49)

NAR.(5): From noon, darkness covered the whole land until three o'clock. Then Jesus cried out with a loud voice:

JESUS: Eloi, Eloi, lema sabachthani?

NAR.(5): My God, my God, why have you forsaken me? Some of the bystanders heard it and said:

1, 4: Listen, he is calling for Elijah.

NAR.(5): Someone ran to fill a sponge with sour wine, put it on a pole, and held it up for Jesus to drink, saying:

2: Wait and see whether Elijah will come take him down.

NAR.(5): Then Jesus, cried with a loud voice.

JESUS: Father, into your hands I commend my spirit.

NAR.(5): And having cried out, he died.
When the centurion saw what had been happening, he praised God.

3: Certainly this man was innocent.

NAR.(5): The crowds who had gathered for the spectacle saw what took place and returned home, beating their breasts, while all his friends, including the women who had followed him from Galilee, stood at a distance, watching.

(Sing:)
In life, no house, no home
My Lord on earth might have;
In death, no friendly tomb
But what a stranger gave.
What may I say? Heav'n was his home;
But mine the tomb wherein he lay.

Here might I stay and sing—
No story so divine!
Never was love, dear King,
Never was grief like thine.
This is my friend, in whose sweet praise
I all my days could gladly spend!

Remembering

Maundy Thursday
First Corinthians 11:23-26

Duration: 12 minutes.

Cast: Mom (also portrays adult Emily)
        Emily (nine years old)
        Grandma
        Grandpa
        Bruce (five years old)

Mom, Grandma, and Grandpa all play to the audience for much of the drama. They should not be thought of as becoming narrators, but as playing to the audience out of their own characters.

Setting: Dining room, with extended areas of stage for bedrooms and bath. Uncovered table is center stage, stretching towards stage right. One chair is center stage at end of table. Two chairs are far stage left.

Props: Could be done totally in pantomime. Props should be kept to minimum and limited to tablecloth (or cloth from Ash Wednesday drama "Dust"), two short candlesticks and candles, box, wrapping paper, and tape.

(MOM and EMILY enter and move directly to the table.)

MOM: *(to audience)* By the time she was approaching her ninth birthday, Emily's young years were filled with plenty of memories.

(MOM and EMILY begin the initial stages of setting a festive table: unfolding, spreading out, and smoothing a tablecloth, and MOM holding plates for EMILY to put on the table.)

EMILY: *(to MOM)* I can remember seven Christmases going all the way back to when I was only three years old and almost pulled the Christmas tree over on myself. I can remember the presents—especially the big ones—and some of the Sunday school programs.

Birthdays kind of get mixed up, except like last year when we had a party and invitation lists and decorations and food to plan.

I can remember when Bruce was born and I was only four. Remember how we painted his room? I really think he's getting too old for the teddy bear wallpaper. I was so excited waiting for him to be born! I just couldn't wait for him to come home from the hospital. *(sighs)* Some days I wonder why. *(pause)* Candles?

MOM: Yes. Get two new yellow ones out of the drawer of the hutch. *(to audience, while EMILY gets out candleholders and candles, unwraps the plastic wrap, etc.)* But of all the memories—routine and special—that Emily holds within herself, there is one set of memories she cherishes beyond anything else and will never let go of.

Two years ago, a great loss came into Emily's life—our lives. It started just after lunchtime, though Emily would not know how much her life had changed until she came home from school. As the children were returning to their classrooms from lunch, everyone heard the sound of a big explosion some distance away that actually shook the windows of her schoolroom. Then they heard the sirens of fire trucks and police cars and ambulances.

When school was out, Emily's teacher asked her to stay behind a moment while everyone else left. She explained that she had gotten a note for the two of them to go to the principal's office. When they got to the principal's office, Gladys Hansen, our next-door neighbor, was there to pick Emily up and bring her home.

GRANDPA: (to audience, entering with GRANDMA from stage left) When they got there, we had just driven in from out of town.

GRANDMA: We're Emily's grandparents.

GRANDPA: Things were in turmoil. There were a couple of police cars and reporters with television cameras. We pushed our way on through.

GRANDMA: Fortunately, Gladys brought Emily in through the back way. She found her mom in the living room in tears.

GRANDPA: All we could do was hold on to each other for a while.

(pause)

GRANDMA: Emily?

MOM: (reaches out to stop GRANDMA) Please. I have to do this myself.

(MOM takes a drink from a glass of water and tries to regain some composure. Then she sits down center stage and takes EMILY on her lap.)

MOM: There was a bad accident at the factory this afternoon—an explosion—in the area where Dad works....Bunches of people were hurt....Two people were killed....Dad was one of them.

(EMILY throws her arms around MOM, and they hold onto each other.)

GRANDMA: (to audience) The next days were a blur for Emily.

GRANDPA: Sometime during those days, we took an old picture of Emily's dad from before she was born, dusted it off, and put it on the mantle.

GRANDMA: Then we found another one for Emily to put in her room, a picture of Emily on a horse at the fair, with her dad standing beside to hold her.

(GRANDMA and GRANDPA hug MOM and EMILY lovingly, then exit stage left.)

MOM: (to audience, as she still sits with EMILY in her lap) How does a young girl manage to hold on to memories of the father she simply aches to see again? She tries to keep track of all the things they did together—the fun things, the funny things, the things she hated to do but now would give anything to do again with Dad. She holds on to memories of going places to-gether—the trips they took, the walks they went on.

(MOM and EMILY return to setting the table.) She cherishes memories of the big things. But more often she remembers the little ones—trips to the grocery store, stopping by the cleaners, walks hand in hand around the block and to the park, kicking the piles of fall leaves.

EMILY: *(to MOM, who now holds a silverware chest as EMILY puts out the pieces around the table)* I can remember how it felt to sit in Dad's lap in the big chair with his big arms around me. I remember stories he told and the books he read to me by the fireplace. I can remember how it felt when Dad would carry me upstairs at night to my room. I remember his tucking me into bed and sitting beside me, his big hand gently rubbing my back until I would fall asleep.

MOM: *(softly coaching Emily as she sets the table)* Turn the knife this way.

EMILY: I remember how I used to wake up at night when that dummy Bruce would call out…

BRUCE: *(offstage)* Dad? Drink?

EMILY: Sometimes I still wake up in the night and try to imagine the sound of Dad's footsteps in the hall…the glow of light from the bathroom…the sound of water running into a glass. I imagine Dad's footsteps going down the hall to Bruce's room, then back again, stopping just a second to peek into my room.

(EMILY and MOM continue to pantomime setting the table.)

GRANDPA: *(To audience, as he and GRANDMA enter stage left and sit on two chairs. They are carrying a box, wrapping paper, and tape, and proceed to wrap the box through the following sequence.)* Holidays were especially hard for everyone; Christmas and Easter were almost unbearable. There would be more people around for holidays than ever before. We would always come up, along with an assortment of aunts, uncles, and cousins.

GRANDMA: Everybody would laugh and joke and do everything they could to keep Emily and Bruce occupied. But Emily would catch us, when we didn't know she was watching, wiping a tear now and then.

MOM: *(to audience)* Emily was born in the spring of the year, late in March. It had become something of a game, called:

EMILY: "How close is my birthday to Easter this year?"

MOM: Tomorrow, when you turn nine years old, will be just a week before Easter. Now, we need to get as many things done ahead of time as we can.

EMILY: Can we set the table for six?

MOM: *(pause, then to audience)* At Emily's first birthday after Dad was gone, she insisted that we set an extra place for him—complete with plate, silver-ware, napkin, wine glass, even a chair—like he might just walk in at any moment and sit down. I have said "No" to doing it at other holidays, but…*(to EMILY)* OK. You can set an extra place.

GRANDMA: *(to audience, as she and GRANDPA come to center from their chairs with the gift)* We drove up on Sunday morning to stay through Easter. We got there about noon, just after they came home from church and Sunday school.

(During this time BRUCE runs in from stage right and hugs GRANDMA.)

GRANDPA: *(to audience)* When we got in the front door, the house already smelled of the roast in the oven. *(to EMILY, as he gives her the present)* We brought a cake, too.

GRANDMA: *(to audience)* In no time at all the roast was out of the oven and the rolls put in to warm. The gravy was made and the potatoes mashed.

EMILY: *(to MOM)* That dummy Bruce—when you gave him the basket of hot rolls from the oven to set on the table—that dummy Bruce went around and put a roll on every plate. On every plate, even on Dad's!

GRANDPA: *(to audience)* Nobody had the nerve to reach over and take it off. So there it sat all by itself while we said grace and all through the whole meal, with everyone sort of ignoring that it was there.

MOM: *(to audience)* When everyone had everything they wanted to eat, and it was time to clear the table and bring out coffee and birthday cake, Emily jumped up to help. *(EMILY picks up "a plate" and exits stage right. BRUCE also skips off right to play.)* She made certain she was the one to remove Dad's plate and once in the kitchen slipped the roll from the plate into her sweater pocket. Then, when the table was clear, she made an excuse to go upstairs. There in her room she took the roll out of her pocket, slipped it under her pillow, and quietly went back downstairs.

(GRANDMA and GRANDPA hug MOM lovingly and exit stage left. She watches them leave. Take this slowly; it is a crucial transition point. MOM is the only one remaining on stage.)

MOM (as adult EMILY): *(slowly turns to the audience)* That was twenty-five years ago, my ninth birthday. It seems like yesterday. *(pause)* The birthday passed and the next day and the next and the next. The dinner roll now had lasted for more than four days already, nestled in a special hiding place in the back of my drawer. Thursday night came and the long Easter weekend was upon us. *(EMILY and BRUCE enter stage right and move "upstairs" to their separate bedrooms.)* Even though there would be no school the next day, my brother and I still got sent to bed early to give the grownups a chance to talk.

(EMILY mimes the actions.) Upstairs, with Bruce safely away in his room, I began my new nightly ritual. I reached into the back of the drawer, took out the slowly shrinking piece of roll, and broke off a tiny piece. Then I turned out the light and snuggled into bed under the covers. With my eyes closed I nibbled on the little piece of bread and thought about my Dad. I could feel him sitting there beside me, softly and gently rubbing my back.

From downstairs the comfortable, far-off, muffled sound of adult voices floated upward as I slowly drifted about on the edge of sleep. *(pause)* All of a sudden I was wide awake!

BRUCE: *(sitting up)* Mom?

EMILY: *(sitting up, speaking to herself)* It's that dummy Bruce! He knows he's old enough to take care of bedtime drinks on his own! Besides, Mom needs time to talk with Grandma and Grandpa without being interrupted!

BRUCE: Mom?

MOM (as adult EMILY): *(EMILY and BRUCE pantomime the actions that follow.)* The pattern was familiar. Bruce would try calling out three times. Then he would either get up and get himself a drink or he would forget it and go to sleep without one. But before Bruce could call out a third time, I threw back *my* covers, and *my* footsteps were the ones going down the hallway. *I* was the one turning on the bathroom light running the water a moment filling a glass. Then *I* went with it down the hallway to Bruce's room.

In the glow of the night-light I could see him sitting up in bed waiting. I handed him the cool water. He took a little sip and handed it back with a sheepish look on his face. Then he flopped back down on the bed and rolled over on his stomach.

I placed the glass on the nightstand and sat down on the bed beside my brother. I sat there quietly for a time…then in the stillness I began to sing. My small voice was clear, but trembling.

EMILY: *(Sings slowly and lightly, taking a deep breath between each phrase.)* "What wondrous love is this, *(breath)* O my soul, O my soul, *(MOM begins speaking line below)*
(breath) What wondrous love is this, *(breath)* O my soul.
(breath) What wondrous love is this…*(continues humming from that point on)*

MOM (as adult EMILY): The only song that came to mind was one we had sung at church on Sunday, a song that had moved through my depths all week long, though I didn't know all the words.

I reached over, gently placed my hand on my brother's back, and began to rub it slowly, remembering how Dad did it. Remembering.

From downstairs the distant, droning voices accompanied my quiet song.

My throat was tight, remembering, inside my chest an enormous weight, remembering.

A great tear rolled off my cheek and dropped onto the bed.

Remembering.

(EMILY's humming continues to the end of the song. There is silence for a time, then the players exit.)

Deliverance

Vigil of Easter: Creation
Genesis 1:1—2:2

Duration: 8 minutes.

Cast: 3 people. A dialog for two persons, perhaps both at reading stands, or sharing the one used by the reader at the beginning.

READER: In the beginning when God created the heavens and the earth, the earth was a formless void and darkness covered the face of the deep, while a wind from God swept over the face of the waters. Then God said, "Let there be light"; and there was light. And God saw that the light was good; and God separated the light from the darkness. God called the light Day, and the darkness he called Night. And there was evening and there was morning, the first day. (Genesis 1:1-5 NRSV)

1: *(reading)* This is the beginning of the mighty acts of deliverance, whereby God…

2: Wait!

1: What's wrong?

2: I thought this was supposed to be the story of creation.

1: It is!

2: But you started out talking about "mighty acts of deliverance."

1: Right. That's what it says here in the script: "mighty acts of deliverance."

2: Something must be wrong with your script! How can the story of God creating the world be called a "mighty act of deliverance?"

1: *(pauses to consider)* You mean like from an eyewitness point of view?

2: I suppose so. There would have to be a deliverance from something or another—like from slavery or oppression or exile—things like that.

1: From an eyewitness point of view.

2: Right.

1: There weren't any.

2: Any what?

1: Eyewitnesses! There were no eyewitnesses of the creation of the universe.

2: Oh. *(stops to think about that)* But suppose there were eyewitnesses. How would it have looked to them?

1: Indescribable!

2: Come again?

1: If there would have been people around to see the creation of the universe or any part of it—and there couldn't have been because people hadn't been created yet—but just pretending there were for your benefit—they would not have had language or concepts sufficient to describe the wonders that were taking place!

2: Like when out of nothingness light suddenly burst forth?

1: Exactly. Even cosmologists today have trouble finding words to express what their mathematics suggest was going on at the beginning of the universe.

2: Or when stars and planets formed in space?

1: Simply too marvelous for words!

2: Plants? Sea creatures? Animals?

1: We may have words and concepts the ancient Hebrews didn't have available to them, but our words and concepts still fall short.

2: But you're right! No one was around to see it happening. No eyewitnesses.

1: Only later would people begin to look back and wonder how it all started and try to imagine.

2: And then, of course, they would bring along their own experiences as they tried to put it into words.

1: Remember, the Hebrew people did have their own experience of God at work throughout their history. What they had experienced of God was deliverance. God brought them out of slavery in Egypt and led them to the promised land. God delivered them again and again from the hands of their enemies. Even when everything seemed lost and hopeless, when the nation was in ruins and the people of Judah were hauled off in captivity to Babylon, God would still deliver them and bring them back to their own land.

2: Then with that kind of history, a "history of salvation," when they would look back at God's work of creation, they would naturally describe it as another—actually the first—*deliverance.*

1: And so, "This is the beginning of the mighty acts of deliverance…"

2: Alright! Alright! I understand! *(pause)* But, how are *we* supposed to look at it?

1: I suppose we can look at it in a lot of different ways. We have a lot of different languages and perspectives we can use to look at the origin of the universe. And all of them have their place. But one of our perspectives—and one of the languages we are going to use—will always come out of our experience of what God has done in human history.

2: Which we know more about than even the ancient Hebrew people did!

1: And that, indeed, is exactly what we are here to celebrate—that the same God who delivered our ancestors in the faith from bondage into freedom is the God who also brings us out of death into life.

2: And both kinds of deliverance are still happening for us day after day, and will continue to happen until our deliverance is final and complete.

1: So, when *we* look back to when everything got started, looking back from what God still continues to do for us—

2: —*we* also find ourselves falling back on the language of deliverance to put it into the perspective of faith.

1: Thus: In the beginning, God delivered the universe from nothingness and brought creation out of chaos.

2: *(testing the new language)* And God delivered stars and planets and galaxies from just being disordered swirling matter and energy?

1: Eventually, God delivered complex living organisms from being non-living matter.

2: And delivered animals with thought processes from being organisms without the ability to think.

1: And finally, brought humankind into the freedom of self-reflection, self-knowledge, choice—

2: —able to look back at ourselves, and ask where we came from and *who* we came from.

1: That is just the beginning of the mighty acts of deliverance whereby God finally brings humankind into freedom and life.

2: Never again will there be nothing!

1: Never again will bondage be final!

2: Never again will death have the last word!

1: So?

2: OK.

1 & 2: This is the beginning of the mighty acts of deliverance whereby God brings humankind into freedom and life.

READER: God saw everything that he had made, and indeed, it was very good. And there was evening and there was morning, the sixth day.

Thus the heavens and the earth were finished, and all their multitude. And on the seventh day God finished the work that he had done, and he rested on the seventh day from all the work that he had done. (Genesis 1:31—2:2 NRSV)

Rainbows

Vigil of Easter: The Flood
Genesis 7, 8, & 9

Duration: 9 minutes.

Cast: Mrs. Noah.

Time: Post-deluge.

Setting: An assembly of people.

READER: Then the Lord said to Noah, "Go into the ark, you and all your household, for I have seen that you alone are righteous before me in this generation."

And Noah with his sons and his wife and his son's wives went into the ark to escape the waters of the flood. (Genesis 7:1, 7 NRSV)

MRS. NOAH: OK.... Well... I... I'm afraid I haven't had much practice at this, at speaking to large assemblies of people. I... In the old days, that is in the days before the great flood, it wasn't customary for women to speak to large groups, and afterwards, well, there weren't any large groups left, so...

Anyway, I'm the one you usually don't hear from. My husband, Noah, gets all the attention; as well he should because he orchestrated the whole thing. But, maybe I can add a little from a different perspective, from someone who also went through it all.

You all know the story of Noah's Ark. Everybody seems to. It's in the Bible and told in countless storybooks as well.

One of the first things most people ask me about is the living conditions in the ark. "Cramped," is the memory that first comes to mind. We had small living quarters, four tiny cabins and a bit larger commons area for cooking and meals and such. The rest was all animals and storage. It was nearly impossible to get away from each other. Oh, we had the whole ark to wander around in, but basically it was like living in a zoo. And wherever one would turn there was some work to be done. This was not a luxury cruise, as you know. It was a means of survival.

We were in the ark for just over a year. Even after the rain stopped, the waters covered everything for a time, and when they subsided we still had to wait for the land to dry. Our food was rationed with care. It had to last us, not only through the time inside the ark, but also until the first harvest.

For the most part, I think we were just all numb at the beginning. There were so many new tasks we had to set our hands to until routine set in. Always there was the incessant drumming of the rain. We learned to tune it out until the noise of the storm broke into our awareness again. I think each of us will always remember the precise moment when suddenly the ark lurched and bobbed, and we knew the waters had risen enough for the ark to float.

He hasn't told this to anyone, but my husband Noah is more of a farmer than a seaman, and he didn't do too well initially with the bobbing and swaying of the boat. I think "a little green around the gills" is your expression for what he was suffering.

The hardest part of that year, however, was not the initial storm. We just gritted our teeth and bore with it. Far harder were those long, long days when we merely floated there upon the water. The trauma was over, and afterwards the deep grief set in for all of us. We finally each had to come to terms with what we had lost. We had all lost loved ones—kinfolk, parents, grandparents, aunts, uncles, cousins. All our families had been left behind except for the eight of us in the ark.

We lost neighbors and the community around us, all of our familiar bearings. Regardless that its time had come and it needed to be gone, it was the world we knew. It had given us some sense of who we were. None of the places we had known would we ever see again—homes, villages. Everything was gone. Nothing would ever be the same.

As we floated upon the water those months, we knew what we had lost and we grieved for it, each in our own way. Some of us wept together, some alone in silence. My three daughters-in-law were a great comfort to me. The men stomped around angry and irritable, rather than admit their tears. You know how they can be. But once I found Noah himself in our cabin sobbing. I felt it best to leave him be.

And so we grieved, as all of you have known grief. The months we spent there upon the waters were not merely time necessary for the waters to subside. *We* needed that time, as well, to grieve our losses. Only when that had taken place could we open the great window of the ark and be ready to hope for the appearance of a new world.

The new world did emerge, a bit at a time. We watched for it day by day. First we saw the mountaintops. Eventually, the new land itself emerged, utterly transformed from before. Then stretches of dry land appeared. Finally, we saw new shoots of green vegetation upon the land. By then our hearts had turned from the old to the new and we were ready to set foot upon the fresh, new world God had provided for us.

What did I think life would be like once we had left the ark? In many ways it would be new, but in other ways it would remain similar to what we had just experienced. There would be the opportunity to start off with a blank slate. How many times do we wish to be able to do that? Well, we could do it! We could try to make things work the way they are supposed to work. We could try out the new, without hesitation. We could try to shape the world the way God intended it.

I also knew that the experience we had just been through would be part of life in our new world, as well. There would be more times coming up when what was old would have to be left behind. We would suffer loss again. We would grieve again. We would have to learn repeatedly that new worlds cannot be embraced when our hands are grasping tightly to the old. Life would continue to be a process of letting go and going on, or once again it would stagnate and become rancid.

That's what the rainbow in the sky reminds me of. It's a sign of hope, but it doesn't appear unless there is rain. The tears of grieving and the ability to hope seem inseparably united. Hope for new opportunities, new possibilities, new perspectives, and new insights can happen only when a place has been prepared for them by letting go of those old things that it's time to discard.

Never forget that rainbows have to do first with rain—with tears—before there can be authentic hope. To hope for the new without being willing to grieve the loss of the old is not hope at all. It is a counterfeit hope, which only succeeds in trapping us where we are. True hope will always be accompanied with some grief, for it reaches out with hands that have let go of something.

Moving through grief towards hope is how change happens. And change is still how humankind moves toward what God intends for us. We can't move ahead until we let go of the past. Death must be accepted if new life is going to begin. That's what the sign of the rainbow means to me—the tears of accepted grief washing our eyes to see clearly the new that God is preparing for us.

Well, I guess that's all I have to say. Thank you for your attention.

We don't have time for questions this evening, but I will anticipate and answer the one that always gets asked. Those months we were holed up in the ark, did it start to smell? Yes, indeed. Like a tomb!

READER: God said, "This is the sign of the covenant that I make between me and you and every living creature that is with you, for all future generations: I have set my bow in the clouds, and it shall be a sign of the covenant between me and the earth. When I bring clouds over the earth and the bow is seen in the clouds, I will remember my covenant that is between me and you and every living creature of all flesh; and the waters shall never again become a flood to destroy all flesh. When the bow is in the clouds, I will see it and remember the everlasting covenant between God and every living creature of all flesh that is on the earth." (Genesis 9:12-16 NRSV)

Heartbreak

Vigil of Easter: The Testing of Abraham
Genesis 22:1-12

Duration: 8 minutes.

Cast: Isaac, the son of Abraham.

Setting: Sometime after the near-sacrifice of Isaac.

READER: After these things God tested Abraham. He said to him, "Abraham!" And he said, "Here I am." He said, "Take your son, your only son Isaac, whom you love, and go to the land of Moriah, and offer him there as a burnt offering on one of the mountains that I shall show you." So Abraham rose early in the morning, saddled his donkey, and took two of his young men with him, and his son Isaac; he cut the wood for the burnt offering, and set out and went to the place in the distance that God had shown him. (Genesis 22:1-3 NRSV)

ISAAC: I couldn't stop myself. The moment the bonds snapped, I leapt free, scattering the kindling in all directions. I shrugged off the cords with pent-up energy and fled away from the horror of the mountaintop.

I ran down the hillside, as fast as my legs could carry me. I was jumping, sprinting, and dodging the scrub-brush. I was leaping boulders, twisting and turning this way and that.

Suddenly, there in front of me, was an unseen, rain-washed gully. My foot slipped. I went down head over heels, tumbling, rolling to a stop.

Cautiously I got up, but pain shot from my ankle. Still I hobbled on, always downhill, as best I could, until I reached a boulder jutting out from the hill-side.

I sat down hard and tried to catch my breath. Carefully, I wiggled my ankle.

From high above, from the brush-hidden hilltop, black smoke plumed off the kindling upon which moments earlier I had been lying. A terrifying climax to those strange, dread-filled days!

Three days earlier, before the sun was up, Abraham, my father, had awakened me and two of the servants. All he would say was that we must be off to make sacrifice to God.

I could tell by his face that something was wrong. Gone was all the love of life I had always seen in my father's face. His face was empty and dead. For three days I kept looking at him to figure out what was going on. For three days he avoided my stares. For three whole days our eyes did not meet.

I kept watching him for some glimmer of the look I had so often seen when he took me out to show me the stars of the sky. I kept watching his eyes for that same look that sometimes came over him when he gazed at me. For three whole days I know he kept watching me; but the moment I would glance at him, he would quickly look away.

We were traveling light for folks off to make sacrifice. We did not have even one prize animal from Abraham's flocks. All my father Abraham would say was, "God will provide."

Did my father hope to find a herdsman along the way with flocks finer than his own? Impossible!

Would my father Abraham even entertain the sacrilege of catching and sacrificing a sick, injured animal straggling alone in the wild? All he would say was, "God will provide."

And that final morning as we left the two servants behind at our camp and set out alone—just the two of us, with Abraham carrying the fire and with the kindling piled high upon my back, but still with no animal for sacrifice—all he would say was "God will provide."

Nevertheless, beneath those confident words I could sense a growing despair in my father. His demeanor had changed from anxious "whistling in the dark" as we left home to "hoping against hope" along the way. Finally, his feelings emerged in sharp, angry rebuke as our footsteps worked their way up the mountainside.

When we reached the mountaintop, he waved me over to the side and insisted I stand by while he labored. I watched him roll stones together, prying them out of the soil if need be. I watched tears running down his face as he fashioned the stones one upon another into a crude rock altar. Then a sob rushed out from his depths as he gathered up in his arms the kindling I had carried and placed it upon the stones.

He picked up the cords that had bound the kindling. Suddenly, a loop of rope snaked out from my father's hands, the same rope tricks he had taught me in order to fell and disable rebellious goats.

But now it was me on the ground, bound helpless by the ropes! Then, I was being lifted up and placed upon the altar. Suddenly, looking up into my father's wild, despairing eyes, I realized the horrible fear long hidden within myself—that someday Abraham's God, too, would require of him nothing less than did the gods of the peoples around us.

I turned my ankle carefully to test it. From far up the hillside the voice of my father startled me, calling out "Isaac." I stumbled to my feet, but pain shot up my ankle again.

"Isaac. Son." Something unexpectedly familiar resonated in the voice calling me. It was not the sullen voice that had journeyed with me the past three days. It was the voice of the father who had held me as a toddler, lifting me high in the air in pride. It was the voice of the father who had taught me how to tend the flocks. It was the voice of the father who used to take me out at night to show me all the stars in the sky. I had not heard that voice for weeks.

"My son," he held his hand out to me.

We finished the descent together. Though he offered me his shoulder, I chose a stout stick to lean upon. He didn't speak a word as we walked. Nor did I. We walked side by side in silence, each with our own thoughts. As probably happens with other fathers and sons, we would never ever talk about that day.

But I will never forget that day, nor could I if I tried! I will always remember three things to my dying day: the feel of the raw wood against my back; the tear-filled, despairing face of my father over me; and the four words he cried out. Yes, I will remember most of all his words as the sharp knife sliced through my binding cords.

And his eyes! Yes, his eyes suddenly gazed upon me as they had all the years of my childhood. Yet, his eyes also looked through me, as if still focused upon the deepest mystery of the universe. His eyes did not blink, as out of the depths of his own soul Abraham sobbed his universe-shattering exclamation:

"God's heart breaks, too!"

READER: Then the angel of the Lord said to Abraham, "...*now* I know that you truly fear the Lord..."

Freedom

Vigil of Easter: Israel's Deliverance
Exodus 14

Duration: 9 minutes.

Cast: One or two people can do this narrative. The characters relate the experience of the deliverance of the people of Israel from Pharaoh's army. If done by one person alone, that person simply does both parts.

READER: Then the LORD said to Moses: Tell the Israelites to turn back and camp in front of Pi-hahiroth (pai-huh-HAI-rahth), between Migdol and the sea, in front of Baal-zephon (BAY-uhl-ZEE-fuhn); you shall camp opposite it, by the sea. Pharaoh will say of the Israelites, "They are wandering aimlessly in the land; the wilderness has closed in on them." I will harden Pharaoh's heart, and he will pursue them, so that I will gain glory for myself over Pharaoh and all his army; and the Egyptians shall know that I am the LORD. And they did so. (Exodus 14:1-4 NRSV)

1: I don't think I have words to convey sufficiently to you the horror of that night. There is no doubt in my mind that it was the most terrifying experience that any of us would ever have.

2: It was worse by far than that other night of terror just a few short days before. That earlier night we huddled inside our huts in Egypt behind door frames splashed with the blood of the lambs we killed. We then prepared to eat those lambs that same night, with bitter herbs and unleavened bread. Our shoes were on our feet and we were packed up, ready to go.

1: I remember the silence of that night after we had eaten. We sat in absolute stillness, for we had been told the angel of death would pass over the entire land. Only we who sat behind the bloodstained doorposts would be safe.

2: First there was stillness. Then in the distance we heard the screams of discovery—the moaning and the wailing that filled the night—as those not spared discovered their firstborn lifeless.

1: Finally, the Egyptians were ready to be rid of us! No more hesitation! Now they were ready to drive us out, to bribe us with gold and jewels to leave their land.

2: And so we went, for we were ready, following our leader Moses. A disorganized lot, off we went with whatever we could carry or haul on carts. We didn't want to lose a moment for fear our masters would change their minds and forbid it.

1: We tried to stay close to next of kin and keep our children near our side. In that confusion, if any got separated it would be days before they were reunited.

2: We had little time for deeper considerations, yet we all wondered inside ourselves just who we were now. We were still the Hebrew people. We were still slaves, slaves on the run. But on the run to what? We were constantly looking over our shoulders to see our masters in pursuit.

1: And so we moved forward out of Egypt. We were a huge mass of people with only one goal: to distance ourselves from that land. In the daytime we moved forward, by night we camped. Moses and our leaders tried to find a way into the wilderness that would not leave us trapped, with an Egyptian army outpost before us and a pursuing army behind us.

2: Yet, in all of that mass departure, the real terror had not even begun. That horror began the night we camped up against the marshy Sea of Reeds to our east and looked back to the west. There, on the rise behind us, silhouetted against the twilight sky, from north to south as far as the eye could see, stood the whole army of Pharaoh.

1: We huddled in our makeshift tents and shelters, convincing each other that the army of Egypt would not attack in the darkness. When early morning light came, we knew they would swoop down upon us. Would we resist? Of course we would, with staves and sticks, butchers knives, maybe a sword or two. But we were slaves and they were an army.

2: In the end we believed they would murder and rape and haul our children back to Egypt into a worse lot than we had known. And so we huddled in terror, not even noticing the steady wind that had arisen from the east and that would keep growing and growing.

1: How do you spend your last night alive? Do you lie awake, relishing every passing moment? Or do you try to sleep a dreamless sleep to let the last hours slip away or to gain energy for a futile fight? Even such final requests of those about to die were denied to us by the wind—the insidious wind that only grew in intensity. It grew until our tents and shelters were collapsing. It grew as we tried to hold onto our belongings and keep them from blowing back to Egypt. It grew as the dust and sand penetrated our clothing, our eyes, and our mouths.

2: We hugged the ground, trying to hold down our possessions and hold onto each other, shutting our eyes against the sand, trying to breathe through shawls and headpieces against the dust. Still the wind grew until we forgot the Egyptians and despaired of surviving the storm raging around us.

1: Then, when we were certain we could no longer endure, the word began to flow through the camp: "Get up! Move out! Grab what you can! Flee to the east, into the wind, into the marsh!"

2: There was nothing else to do. We had to get up and move out or be trampled by the rest. So, we were up, clutching our belongings, trying to lead what animals we had among us, holding onto our children. We pushed to the east, into the wind, our faces shielded against it. We went into the wind, into the darkness, into the marshy waters, but for what purpose?

1: Surrounded by the swirling noise of wind and the cries of frightened people, I concentrated on not falling and being trampled. It was some time before I realized I was no longer trudging through the sand. I was walking upon crusty ground, dark crusty soil such as you see in a dried up lake bed.

2: Bit by bit we realized we were already far into the marsh, the marsh grasses trampled down by those ahead of us, the crusty soil turning into dust under foot. And our feet were dry!

1: I don't know how long we pushed on through the dry marsh bottom, still fighting the assault of the wind before us. I lost all track of time. Eventually, we felt the land begin to rise under our feet, then the crusty marsh bottom turned again to sand.

2: Still we pushed forward, upward, simply to avoid falling under the feet of those following behind us. Finally, exhausted, no longer pressured by those coming behind, we fell to the ground, with no strength left in our bones.

1: There we waited, too weary to rise, as the first light of dawn grew in the eastern sky. We waited for the army of Pharaoh to mobilize, to swoop down into the valley and across the dry marsh as easily as we had. So weary with the terror of that night and fearful of the prospects of the new day, we did not even notice that the wind had stopped perfectly still.

2: Through the earth we could feel the thunder of horses' hooves and in the distance we could hear the clank of chariots and armor. Then the cries began at the edge of our people on the shore nearest the marsh. The slaughter had begun. It would be only a matter of time before it reached us. No one had the strength any longer to rise and resist.

1: Slowly across the camp the cries grew—and only slowly did we begin to realize that what we were hearing were cries of joy, shouts of exuberance. As that realization unfolded across the camp, we found the energy again to rise and look back to the west, into the marsh from our higher ground.

2: There stood the whole army of Egypt—but still in the marsh, not upon our shore. Their chariot wheels and horses' hooves had broken through the crusty bottom that had sustained our whole company. All of Pharaoh's host was mired down, sinking deeper and deeper into the muddy bottom, while the waters, without the wind to hold them back, surged forward upon the Egyptians.

1: Now our whole camp was on its feet, cheering and shouting and leaping into the air. All of our weariness was gone as we realized what all this meant: We were no longer slaves! We would never be slaves again! We were free! Free! Free!

READER: Thus the Lord saved Israel that day from the Egyptians; and Israel saw the Egyptians dead on the seashore. Israel saw the great work that the Lord did against the Egyptians. So the people feared the Lord and believed in the Lord and in his servant Moses. (Exodus 14:30-31 NRSV)

Can These Bones Live?

Vigil of Easter: The Valley of the Dry Bones
Ezekiel 37:1-14

Duration: 8 minutes

This drama is really only a framework and an invitation for the actors to become writers. Part One should remain as it is. Parts Two through Four are very specific to this author and are an invitation to write copy specific to the actors. Part Two comes from the author's own personal experiences. Part Three comes out of the recent memory of the author's community. Part Four is specific to the author.

Cast: One or two people can do this narrative. If done by one person alone, that person simply does both parts.

Props: The "bones" indicated in this drama are imaginary.

READER: The hand of the LORD came upon me, and he brought me out by the spirit of the LORD and set me down in the middle of a valley; it was full of bones. He led me all around them; there were very many lying in the valley, and they were very dry. (Ezekiel 37:1-2 NRSV)

PART ONE

(1 and 2 begin walking around the chancel area.)

1: Bones! Bones! As far as the eye can see, bones! Nothing but bones! A valley filled with bones! White bones, bleached by the sun. And very dry.

2: Here are the bones of ancient Israel—the bones of those indeed slaughtered before the advancing armies of Babylon. Here are the bones of those who died of famine or disease in the siege of Jerusalem. Here are the bones of those carried away to die in Babylon, among them the bones of King Zedekiah—his eyes put out after being forced to witness the slaughter of his sons.

1: *(moves to a new area)* And here lie the bones of Israel from another time and another place, from times and places we still remember: Auschwitz, Dachau. They are the bones of the six million Jews. And here are bones of yet another six million—gays, gypsies, the physically or mentally handicapped, voices of protest—all of them considered objectionable, expendable.

2: *(moves to a new place)* Here are the bones left behind by the crusades, by all of humankind's crusades. And here lie the bones left by the scourge of the black plague in Europe, and by all the plagues of humankind.

1: *(moves to another spot)* And these are the bones of battlegrounds whose names are still known to us: Gettysburg, Normandy, Nanking, Hiroshima, Viet Nam, Central America, Rwanda, Kosovo…

2: Nothing but bones! A whole valley of bones! Dry bones.

PART TWO

1: *(stoops down to pick up a bone, then stands)* She was young and beautiful and full of life. She was a working artist by profession, and I still have a couple of her sketches. Along with her husband, she was a fine musician. Together with some other folks we made a lot of wonderful music.

With her seizures under medical control, all of life lay ahead of her. Her life lay ahead of her until that early morning when she rose while her husband was still asleep, ran a tub full of water for her bath, then was suddenly, unexpectedly overcome by a seizure. She tumbled forward into the tub and drowned.

Kathy. *(gently places the bone back on the ground and stays in squatting position)*

2: *(looks around and picks up another bone, then stands)* He could have been a college freshman this year. My last memory of Nathan is of him sitting in his infant carrier on top of my huge desk in my campus ministry office. Nathan had come as a surprise to my part-time secretary and her husband, just as she was finishing up a masters program. But they received him as the gift that he was, along with some modification of their plans. I said, "I would love to have you continue working here part-time, if you would like. And don't worry about child care. We have a lot of space here in the center, and we're very casual. Just bring him along."

And so Nathan sat on my desk that day, and we conversed about the deeper things of the universe, while his mom quickly ran some materials to the printer. The next morning, a Maundy Thursday, the tragic phone call came: "We had to rush Nathan to the hospital early this morning. He won't be coming home again, ever."

Undertakers provide Styrofoam coffins for infants. Nothing in all the world seems as light as a baby's casket. It is as if it could lift up and float away on the slightest breeze. *(lays that bone down carefully and stays in squatting position)*

1: *(moves to another area, picks up another bone, stands, pauses, then takes a deep breath)* Our lives were bound together for twenty-four years. I'm sure I have inherited many of his mannerisms: his compassion and tender heart, and very likely some of his scares and fears. He lived long enough to meet the woman I would marry, but died before the wedding took place. He would never know his grandsons, not even as children. *(places that bone down, then stays in squatting position)*

2: *(hunts around, picks up another bone, stands, pauses again, then takes a very deep breath)* So tiny. So very tiny. We would have named her...No. I better not go there. *(takes another deep breath, pauses, then places the bone down tenderly, and stays in squatting position)*

1: (reaches out for another bone, then stands) She was seven years older than me, so growing up as children we were never really companions. We grew close after we both became adults. Her first love was church music, which began in seventh grade when she started accompanying the liturgy and hymns on a piano in our family's country church in rural Iowa. She went to Valparaiso University for a year and studied organ and sang in the chapel choir. Over the decades, separated by distance, we kept in touch mostly over the telephone. Always, perhaps after first exchanging gossip about relatives, our conversation turned to church music.

When you sign up to be a pastor there are things you don't anticipate you might someday do, like conducting the graveside service for your sister, there on a hillside in rural Iowa, overlooking the church where she first led God's people in worship. (lays down bone carefully and stays in squatting position)

PART THREE

2: (moves over a ways and picks up several bones, then stands) These three would be nurses now, if it had not been for that icy highway. (lays the bones down and stays in squatting position)

1: (picks up another, then stands) Kevin, who drowned over spring break a few years ago, with his family at Cancun. (lays the bone down and stays in squatting position)

2: (picks up another, then stands) And another icy highway just a year ago. (lays that bone down and stays in squatting position)

1: (picks up another, then stands) The house fire last summer. (lays down the bone and stays in squatting position through final reading)

PART FOUR

2: (stands and steps back, slightly tripping, then reaches down and picks up the bone he was tripping over) Born during the Second World War, he would grow up and enter the ministry as a young adult. Nearly all of his ministry would be spent as a campus pastor, first in Omaha, then later at Valparaiso…(drops the bone, like it has singed his fingers)

Oh, my God, we are all bones. Nothing but bones. Dry bones, white and bleached by the sun, and very, very dry. (slumps down to the ground and remains through final reading)

READER: Thus says the Lord GOD: Come from the four winds, O breath, and breathe upon these slain, that they may live.

I am going to open your graves, and bring you up from your graves, O my people; . . . And you shall know that I am the LORD, when I open your graves, and bring you up from your graves, O my people. I will put my spirit within you, and you shall live, and I will place you on your own soil; then you shall know that I, the LORD, have spoken and will act, says the LORD. (Ezekiel 37:9b, 12b-14 NRSV)

Reunion

Second Sunday of Easter
John 20:19-31

Duration: 10 minutes.

Setting: A rehearsal for a dramatic portrayal of the story of Thomas and the Easter appearances of Jesus.

Cast: Director
        Andy, who portrays the disciple Andrew
        Jim, who portrays the disciple James
        Phil, who portrays the disciple Philip
        Pete, who portrays the disciple Peter
        Tom, who portrays the disciple Thomas
        Jay, who portrays Jesus

The Director should be played by a woman. If a racially mixed cast is available, Tom should be played by someone who is a visually distinctive minority compared to the majority of the cast.

(ANDY, JIM, PHIL, PETE, and JAY are lounging around in the front of the worship space, on the chancel steps, if available.)

(enter DIRECTOR)

DIRECTOR: OK. Look alive. We'll start right off working on scene three.

ANDY: Tom's not here yet. Can't do scene three without Tom.

DIRECTOR: Well, where is he? It's already late.

JIM: Oh, that's just the way Tom is.

PHIL: He's always been…Oh, you know…He has this attitude!

JIM: Probably hanging out with his friends. He's never been, well, really one of us.

ANDY: Always been different. "Cultural differences?" *(the others laugh)*

PETE: Think we should give him a phone call?

JIM: I think Tom needs to take responsibility for himself.

DIRECTOR: OK, OK. We're wasting time. Let's start with scene one instead. We don't need Tom for scene one. It's got some rough spots in it as well.

(Cast stands and "takes places.")

DIRECTOR: *(sarcastically)* Is everyone here for scene one?

ANDY: Yup. All ten of us. *(the others laugh)* Well that's what we're supposed to be: the ten disciples.

PETE: I thought there were twelve disciples.

ANDY: There were at one time. We're down to ten.

JAY: There would actually have been thirteen of them with Jesus, who was really the reason for the other twelve getting together.

PHIL: That's right. There would always have been thirteen of them wherever they went.

JIM: Restaurant managers had to cringe seeing them coming!

ANDY: *(holding imaginary clipboard, to PHIL)* Can I help you, sir?

PHIL: *(to ANDY)* Table for thirteen, please.

(ANDY throws imaginary clipboard over his shoulder.)

DIRECTOR: OK, OK. Let's get into it. You're not thirteen any longer. Jesus has been excluded—by crucifixion.

(JAY moves center stage, sits down, hunched over with his head down, making himself as small as possible. Disciples position themselves in front of him, effectively hiding him from view.)

Now it's three days later, and even his body is missing. Take it from there.

ANDY: And, don't forget—Judas would no longer be with them either.

JAMES (Jim): So what got into Judas? He was the last person I thought would betray Jesus.

PETER (Pete): He didn't just betray Jesus. He betrayed all of us. This is the first time we've even managed to get back together since that night in the garden.

PHILIP (Phil): I heard he did it for money.

ANDREW (Andy): Well, I don't think we'll be seeing any more of him.

PETER (Pete): Right. He went out afterwards and killed himself.

OTHERS: What?

PETER (Pete): That's the word I got. He hung himself.

DIRECTOR: Remember, this is the first some of you have heard of it, so it comes as a shock. You have barely gotten over the fact that he excluded himself from your company by betraying all of you. Now you hear that he has, "excluded himself from himself," so to speak. Therefore, express shock! OK, go on.

ANDREW (Andy): And where's Thomas. Anybody seen him?

JAMES (Jim): Oh, you know how Thomas is.

PHILIP (Phil): He's always been…Oh, you know…He has this attitude!

JAMES (Jim): Probably hanging out with his friends. He's never been, well, really one of us.

ANDREW (Andy): Always been different. "Cultural differences?"

PETER (Pete): Think we should try to find him?

JAMES (Jim): He can take care of himself.

(Suddenly, JESUS stands up behind the disciples, a step or two up on the chancel steps, if available, or perhaps on a stool. He towers over them.)

DIRECTOR: Now, remember what's happening here. You are keenly aware of who's missing from your company. Well, this is the number one excluded one. He was excluded from the religious establishment. The political establishment felt it was expedient for him to be crucified. He was excluded by all of you, who ran away when the going got tough. He was excluded even by God.

JESUS (Jay): *(spreading his arms in cruciform fashion)* My God, my God, why have your forsaken me?

DIRECTOR: Suddenly, the excluded one stands among you again. React!

(Disciples react in various ways as they turn toward JESUS.)

JESUS (Jay): *(relaxing from cruciform stance to exhibit his hands in a welcoming gesture)* Peace be with you! Shalom! Wholeness, healing, be with you!

(Actors hold the scene for a moment.)

TOM: *(breaking in from side)* Yo. I made it!

PETE: Well, it's about time. We had to go on without you.

TOM: Sorry.

ANDY: Let's see, this time it was your mom who got sick and you had to take her to the emergency room.

TOM: I had…

PHIL: Your dog ran off, and you've been looking all over for him.

DIRECTOR: Tom, we had to go back and work on the first scene. But, if you had been any later, I'm afraid I was getting ready to write myself into your part. I think I could muster up the feelings of one who gets left out. OK, we can polish up scene one next time. Let's skip to scene three.

(The disciples regroup, THOMAS among them and JESUS again takes "hidden" position behind disciples.)

Now regardless of what they may have felt about Thomas's absence, over the next week (which was scene two), those feelings are overcome by the wonder of Jesus' resurrection, and they do get the word to Thomas. Thus, in scene three, a week later, Thomas shows up, even though he's skeptical about the whole thing and has told them as much.

(Disciples group around THOMAS, some back slapping and mimed exclamations of what they had seen. THOMAS shakes his head incredulously.)

(Slowly, JESUS rises to full standing position behind them. As he does so all but THOMAS notice and turn, stepping slightly to the side to leave space open between JESUS and THOMAS, front center. THOMAS, however, ends

up facing away from JESUS and only late turns to discover the risen JESUS standing among them, some feet away from THOMAS.)

DIRECTOR: Careful here with what's going on. Though Thomas is seeing Jesus for the first time, it's not as big a surprise for the rest. What has to be on their mind, and on Thomas's mind, is the question of how Jesus is going to treat Thomas, who first had absented himself and then refused to believe what the others had seen. Will Jesus ignore Thomas? Give him the cold shoulder? Scold him? Put him down?

(Pause, to let the questions linger. Then, JESUS spreads out his hands to show his wounds and walks forward to THOMAS. One by one JESUS takes THOMAS's hands and puts his fingers upon the wounds in JESUS' hands. Then JESUS embraces THOMAS and THOMAS returns the embrace. Actors hold the scene for a moment.)

DIRECTOR: OK. Cut. Good. Now, we're supposed to have a discussion with the audience after each performance. So. What do you think was going on?

(Actors sit on the chancel steps, if available, or on chairs or stools at the front of the worship space.)

ANDY: I think there's something here that says that the Easter faith is not just marching around yelling, "Alleluia." It has to do with our relationships with other people.

JIM: Right. I think Jesus is telling us that after what happened at Easter nobody is to be excluded ever again.

ANDY: Nobody written off. You know, "That's the way he is . . . That's the way she is . . ."

DIRECTOR: "Men are so . . ."

PHIL: "Women are so . . ."

JIM: You can fill in the blanks with all the ways we write people off—color, class, culture, age, religion. Easter means that the time for that kind of thinking is over.

TOM: Like what happened this evening when my car wouldn't start . . .

JAY: Your car wouldn't start?

TOM: Yeah. Battery was dead. That's why I was late.

JAY: I didn't know that. *(pause)* Then part of our Easter faith is not only *not* writing each other off; we also need to listen to each other. I was so caught up in my own story that I didn't think of Tom having his own story. But without it, all I have is my story, never our story.

TOM: And then we need to add in everybody else's story as well, to make it really *our* story.

PETE: And on and on and on, until eventually every story is woven together, which probably isn't going to be complete until the final Easter.

JAY: But the first Easter tells us to get going on the process.

DIRECTOR: I'm glad you got here, Tom. We probably could have made do without you, but without you we would have been diminished. We would have been something less without you!

JAY: Which is another piece of the Easter faith. Without each other we are not whole. Didn't Jesus come back wishing them "Shalom," which is not simply peace, but wholeness?

PETE: We can't have wholeness without each other. I need people of other races and colors and backgrounds and cultures and religions…

JAY: Blacks and whites and Asians and Native Americans, Serbs and Albanians *[change this ethnic reference as world conditions change]*, Jewish folk and Muslims—without each other we are less than whole. That wholeness may take a lot of work, but it's the direction our Easter faith takes us.

ANDY: So, the story ends happily! Jesus and the disciples are all reunited!

JIM: Not so fast there. The ten became eleven, then the eleven became twelve, *but…*

PHIL: Judas! What about Judas?

JAY: Oh, dear God!

JIM: Yes! Dear God, what about Judas?

Window on God

Fourth Sunday of Easter
John 10; Psalm 23

Duration: 11 minutes.

Setting: a meeting of a small, congregational committee to select and recommend a new stained glass window for their church. The cast could sit at a short table with four chairs (two in back and one on each end), or they could sit in four folding chairs in a semi-circle.

Cast: Judith (50 years old, chairperson)
Sarah (late teens or young adult)
David (35 years old)
Elmer (70 years old)

Props: Four manila folders with a few sheets of paper in them and a large rolled up paper.

(The cast comes forward to take their seats. JUDITH is carrying a pack of four manila folders. ELMER has a large rolled up sheet of paper.)

JUDITH: Will the meeting of the First Lutheran New Millennium Ad Hoc Chancel Beautification Committee please come to order.

DAVID: Couldn't we just call it the Stained Glass Window Committee?

JUDITH: Well, I don't know. We might have more tasks assigned to us.

DAVID: I don't think so. The council just wants a recommendation for a stained glass window. Besides, that's all I signed on for—one meeting, two at the most.

JUDITH: *(sighs)* OK, then. Will the Stained Glass Window Committee please come to order. I think we all know each other. Do you gentlemen both know Sarah? She's representing the youth of the congregation.

DAVID: Yeah. I know Sarah from choir.

ELMER: *(shakes hands with SARAH)* Glad to meet you, Sarah.

JUDITH: Now, I think we all know why we are here. I have prepared some folders of materials for each of us. *(distributes manila folders)* Inside, first of all, is a copy of the letter regarding the memorial gift which will fund the window, leaving the selection of the window up to the congregation. I also got some brochures from a couple of stained glass window companies and included them to start us thinking. OK? Now, since Elmer builds things, I asked him in advance to check on the feasibility of putting a stained glass window into the wall of the chancel. Elmer?

ELMER: Well, I wasn't around here when they built this new sanctuary maybe 35 years ago, but I was able to find the blueprints. *(unrolls the paper on the table for everyone to see)* It looks like they planned to eventually put a window in the chancel someday. Probably couldn't afford it when it was first under construction. But, see, there's this header here. That's like a beam to support the weight above it. So all one has to do is go through the wall and stick in a window. No structural problems at all. *(rolls the paper back up and others go back to looking through their folders)*

JUDITH: So, that means all we have to do is select a window and make a recommendation to the council.

SARAH: *(paging through a brochure in her folder)* There's some beautiful windows here—Saint Peter…Saint Paul…Saint Timothy…

DAVID: Yes, Sarah, that would be fine if we were named after Peter or Paul or Timothy, or after some other saint. But, we're First Lutheran Church.

SARAH: *(muses for a moment)* So how about a window with a great big number one?

(DAVID and ELMER groan.)

JUDITH: Actually, being named First Lutheran leaves us open to almost anything. It's not like we were stuck having to have a certain saint or the Good Shepherd or…

DAVID: But how about that? The Good Shepherd. You know, I still remember my first impressions of that from the church we went to when I was a very small child. Actually, we moved away from there on my fourth birthday, so I really was very little. Anyway, I can still remember sitting in that little white, wood-frame church building, on the hard pew, and looking up at the stained glass window. They only had one. It was high up on the wall of the chancel and not very big. There was only room for two sheep, and they weren't completely in the picture, standing at the feet of Jesus, who was holding a lamb in his arms. My mother always told me that the name of the lamb was "David."

SARAH: That's neat! I like that!

DAVID: Sometime later, when I learned to sing "I am Jesus' little lamb," it came as no news to me. I felt like I had always known it. I guess that was where my faith started. Jesus was my Good Shepherd, and I knew Jesus and God were just like that. *(holds up two intertwined fingers)* So, God was also my Good Shepherd.

ELMER: Not a bad place for anybody's faith to start!

JUDITH: But, I'm certain that was not where your faith ended! And we are not a congregation of small children. Perhaps we deserve an image with a greater degree of theological sophistication for this congregation. There are a number of abstract images included in one of these catalogs that show fine artistic sensitivities.

SARAH: This one looks like a boat.

ELMER: Probably a symbol for some apostle.

SARAH: Maybe you're right. Maybe we need something abstract. There are a lot of professional people in the congregation—doctors, lawyers, business owners, teachers. And everybody in my generation is in college or planning to go to college. We're all pretty independent and stand on our own feet. We're competent in a lot of different ways. That's not in the least the way I picture sheep. And, I don't think that I aspire to be a sheep.

DAVID: I still like the idea of the Good Shepherd.

JUDITH: We're not rejecting the idea of a Good Shepherd window. We're just setting it aside to explore other possibilities.

ELMER: The same way we do with Jesus as the Good Shepherd? As we grow up, we don't reject the idea, we just keep it filed away somewhere.

DAVID: That's a good file to keep around, as far as I'm concerned. You never know when you might need to get your hands on it.

SARAH: *(reading)* "The Lord is my Shepherd. I shall not want. He makes me to lie down in green pastures. He leads me beside the still waters…" They have the twenty-third psalm printed out here on this page with a couple of Good Shepherd windows. Sounds so quiet and peaceful.

ELMER: If only life was always like that! Read on; you'll get to the part about the valley of the shadow of death.

DAVID: That valley is never far away from us, I'm afraid. We ought to be aware of that, from listening to the prayers on Sunday mornings. Pastor does a pretty good job of keeping track of those in the congregation who are walking through that valley in someway or another. Illnesses. Deaths. Folks being hospitalized for tests. Long-term health problems. Sometimes other things.

JUDITH: And there are a lot of things pastor knows about members that don't get into our Sunday prayers—broken relationships, betrayals, broken hearts, people's hopes and dreams getting crushed. We hear such things only in generalities, but some of our folks are actually walking that valley of the shadow of death in a whole variety of different ways.

SARAH: I was just thinking about all the communities that have been affected by gun violence recently. You better believe the twenty-third psalm and the Good Shepherd play pretty well in those communities.

ELMER: Sooner or later we all need the Good Shepherd.

DAVID: Sometimes sooner, rather than later.

JUDITH: But the question we have to deal with right now is whether we want the Good Shepherd there in front of us all the time, looking down at us from high on the chancel wall.

ELMER: Matter of fact, Judith, the Good Shepherd is there for us all of the time. That's part of his goodness, his faithfulness. Whether at the moment the image is "on file" or we are clinging to it for dear life, the Good Shepherd will be there.

SARAH: That's the Good News, I guess, about the Good Shepherd!

DAVID: And whether we have the image before us in a window or not, the Good Shepherd is the one who has brought us into his flock. Like the twenty-third psalm says, he even sets a table before us here—at least in the presence of our friends. Maybe sometimes even in the presence of our enemies.

SARAH: I kind of like the idea of being reminded of that every time I walk into church.

DAVID: And it fits because we gather to hear his word, and the Shepherd is the one whose voice we know and who calls us by name. There's a lot of comfort in that.

ELMER: Don't forget that the Shepherd doesn't just comfort. Sometimes he has to prod us—when we get too near the edge of a cliff, or wander too close to the wolf, maybe even end up down some dead-end gully away from the flock.

SARAH: Maybe that's what it means here, *(reading)* "Your *rod* and your *staff* they comfort me."

DAVID: But the bottom line is this—nothing will ever snatch us out of his hands.

JUDITH: I think you've nearly convinced me. It doesn't seem to be a matter of "sooner or later we all need the Shepherd," but finally the Shepherd will be the only thing we have. Maybe it wouldn't be such a bad idea to have that fact staring us in the face, no matter how sophisticated and unlike sheep we might feel at any moment.

ELMER: Let me tell you, since I'm further along than the rest of you. It hasn't happened yet, but the day is going to come when my independence is going to fade, and all the abilities I am so proud of will have run their course, and even all the knowledge of my faith will evaporate. That could all happen over a long, painful, period of time, or in a sudden flash. It could happen to you before it happens to me. Whenever and however it happens, we finally all end up with absolutely nothing left—except the Shepherd.

DAVID: *(staring up as if back in his childhood church)* You know, I can still see that window from when I was a child, with those two sheep because that's all the room there was—and them not even completely in the picture—standing at the foot of Jesus who is holding in his arms a lamb whose name I knew. I guess that isn't a bad place for anybody's faith to begin!

SARAH: *(reaching out with her hand and placing it on ELMER's shoulder)* And it's not a bad place for anyone's faith to end. *(SARAH and ELMER hug)*

Waiting

Pentecost
Acts of the Apostles 1 and 2

Duration: 10 minutes.

Setting: Jerusalem guest house, the day before Pentecost.

Cast: Mary (the mother of Jesus, 45–50 years old)
Thomas (30–35 years old)
Andrew (30–35 years old)
James (30–35 years old)
Peter (30–35 years old)

Props: A chair or stool, a large book and a large loaf of fresh-baked bread. (Wrapped securely in clear plastic wrap, the loaf could be used later for Holy Communion.)

(THOMAS is alone on stage, pacing back and forth. Eventually he sits down on a chair or stool, picks up a large book, and attempts to read, paging around for a bit. Finally, he tosses the book to the floor, gets up, and starts pacing again. Let this action last for perhaps 45 seconds.)

MARY: *(enters)* Thomas?

THOMAS: What? Oh, hi, Mary!

MARY: What's going on?

THOMAS: Nothing…*(goes back to pacing, then, frustrated)* Waiting! *(paces)* Waiting, that's what's going on. That's all that's going on!

MARY: Where is everyone else?

THOMAS: Oh, they're around somewhere. I suppose they're all off trying to kill time. Andrew went out to get some fresh bread. Should be back any moment. I'm afraid this guest house is getting a little small for all of us. Well, to be honest, we really have started getting on each other's nerves.

MARY: I can imagine!

THOMAS: *(paces more, then stops)* It's been more than a week now since we were told to stay here and wait! Can't blame people for getting impatient!

MARY: I suppose not.

THOMAS: Anyway, you were wondering where everybody went? *(sighs)* Matthew took off earlier in the week to look up some old friends here in the city to stay with. John and Philip went along. Haven't seen any of them since.

MARY: I'm not sure I trust all of Matthew's old friends.

THOMAS: You can say that again! Finally, this morning, James got concerned and decided to go find them and check things out. Still looking after little brother!

MARY: Who sometimes needs looking after!

THOMAS: *(paces again)* You hear about Peter? He went stomping out of here in a huff yesterday. Said he was tired of waiting and was heading back to Galilee to go fishing. Said the Lord would know were to find him if he wanted him.

MARY: But Jesus said to wait here in Jerusalem!

THOMAS: I know! I know! But the waiting *is* getting to everybody. *(paces)* How are the women doing?

MARY: We're all fine! Salome's family has been extremely gracious and hospitable. And, I suppose women have that built-in patience that God gave us. We're all used to having to wait nine months just to keep the human race going. So, Thomas, why are you still hanging around here?

THOMAS: Remember? I missed out on what was going on once before, on the night after Jesus rose from the dead. I'm not about to do that again! Whatever it is that's supposed to happen, I'm going to be here to see it happen!

(JAMES enters from off stage. THOMAS goes back to pacing, pausing now and then to pay attention to the conversations.)

JAMES: Hi, Mary!

MARY: James! *(they embrace lightly)* Did you find your prodigal brother?

JAMES: Oh, yeah. And Philip and Matthew. They're all caught up playing some new game they learned, rolling dice and moving stones around a circle. Wanted to teach me, but I have better things to do. I am trying to keep track of everyone. Stopped by Salome's. She said you were on your way over here.

MARY: And Peter has taken off, I understand?

JAMES: Yeah. Which really irritates me! He heard Jesus' final command as well as the rest of us: "Wait in Jerusalem for the gift of the Holy Spirit to come upon you."

MARY: Well, one of the first things I learned—you were there at Cana, the wedding—one of the first things I learned was just to do what he said whether or not I understood it!

(ANDREW arrives from off stage with a large fresh-baked loaf of bread under his arm.)

ANDREW: Hey, everybody! You wouldn't believe the way the city is filling up for the festival! I barely got the last loaf of bread. Bakers can't handle the crowd. Hi, Mary.

MARY: Andrew. *(they embrace lightly)*

ANDREW: *(going on as without a pause)* Why, there were Parthians (PAHR-thee-uhnz), Medes (meeds), Elamites (EE-luh-maits), *(pulls out a list)* and residents of Mesopotamia (mehs-oh-poh-TAY-mee-ah), Judea (joo-DEE-ah) and Cappadocia (kap-uh-DOH-shee-uh), Pontus (PAHN-tuhs) and Asia, Phrygia (FRIHG-ee-uh) and Pamphilia (pam-FIHL-ee-uh), Egypt and the parts of Lybia (LIHB-ee-uh) belonging to Cyrene (sai-REE-neh), and visitors from Rome, both Jews and proselytes (PRAHS-uh-laits), Cretans (CREE-tuhns) and Arabs.

THOMAS: You made a list?

ANDREW: Just as I was walking around. Couldn't understand half the languages being spoken on the street. Peter back yet?

JAMES: No, your brother is not back yet!

ANDREW: He will be! Always been like that. Even as a kid. Bet he doesn't get further than Jericho (JEHR-ih-koh). So, what's up?

THOMAS: Nothing. That's the whole problem. Nothing's up. All we're doing is waiting.

ANDREW: Well, if we're waiting for Jesus to send his Spirit upon us, whatever happens is bound to come as a surprise. You can bet on that!

MARY: Life with Jesus was a surprise from the very beginning!

JAMES: And it never stopped being one surprise after another to the very end!

THOMAS: Now I remember what it is I never liked about Jesus. Unpredictable!

JAMES: OK, Andrew, you were first a disciple of John, back when he baptized Jesus, right?

ANDREW: Right. Out by the Jordan River.

JAMES: So, you were there when the Spirit was supposed to have come upon Jesus. What happened?

ANDREW: Well, John told us he saw the Spirit descend like a dove over Jesus. And God had told John that the one on whom he saw the Spirit come would someday baptize with the Holy Spirit.

THOMAS: Did you see it?

ANDREW: I wasn't watching.

THOMAS: Great! But you saw Jesus get baptized. What did he look like? Did he change in some way?

ANDREW: Well, he went in dry and came out wet!

JAMES: Wet?

ANDREW: Wet! You mean did he glow or something? No, he was just wet. Eventually he dried off!

THOMAS: This is getting us nowhere! We're waiting around for something to happen and we don't even know what we're waiting for.

ANDREW: OK, Mary, didn't the angel who told you that you would give birth to Jesus say that the Holy Spirit would come upon you? Do you remember what that was like?

MARY: Oh, Andrew, I was so young and scared. I don't remember much of anything. I didn't even know what to expect as signs I was carrying a child. My mother had to tell me what to watch for. And sure enough, pretty soon all the signs were there. But it all took place very quietly. We just had to wait and be patient.

JAMES: Waiting and being patient seems to be what everyone is having so much trouble with!

MARY: Then stop waiting. I mean, just get on with life. We can stay right here in Jerusalem and still get on with life. Tomorrow is the Harvest Festival. People have been traveling days and weeks to get here for it. You still have that list, Andrew? *(ANDREW pats his pocket)* Here we are right in the middle of Jerusalem, so busy "waiting" for something that we could miss the whole festival.

JAMES: OK, then, let's get everybody back together for it. I think I know how to track everyone down. We'll gather here before sundown. We'll share Andrew's bread. Then we'll read from the Law, the appropriate parts, and read the book of Ruth.

ANDREW: And tomorrow we can all gather here again first thing in the morning and go to the temple for the celebration, though I don't know how close we can get with all the crowds.

JAMES: We'll have to leave early.

MARY: And afterwards, Salome's family wants us all over to their place for a meal. Right, all of us. The women have been helping them prepare for it all week. We qualify as the "strangers in town" for their holiday hospitality.

(enter PETER, perhaps down center aisle)

THOMAS: Well, look who's coming!

ANDREW: Hey, little brother!

JAMES: Peter!

(Greeting and back slapping all around. MARY comes and gives PETER a hug.)

ANDREW: I knew you'd be back!

PETER: Oh, I got as far as Jericho.

ANDREW: *(to others)* What did I tell you?

PETER: All the traffic was going the other way, back to Jerusalem. I said, "What am I doing? I'm going to miss out on the festival!" So, I spent the night in Jericho and headed back at dawn.

MARY: We're glad you're back with us, Peter. In fact, we're just planning for the celebration tonight and tomorrow.

PETER: Good, I'm glad I came back—though I'm not making any promises for how long. OK? *(pauses, as if startled by something)* Woah! *(shivers)* Wow! What was that?

THOMAS: Oh, it's nothing. Merely the wind coming up!